PIANO DUET PLAY-ALONG

VOLUME 32

1 PIANO, 4 HANDS

SONDHEIM F[OR TWO]

ISBN 978-1-4234-7289-6

HAL•LEONARD® CORPORATION

7777 W. BLUEMOUND RD. P.O. BOX 13819 MILWAUKEE, WI 53213

Visit Hal Leonard Online at
www.halleonard.com

CONTENTS

BEING ALIVE
from COMPANY

SECONDO

Music and Lyrics by
STEPHEN SONDHEIM

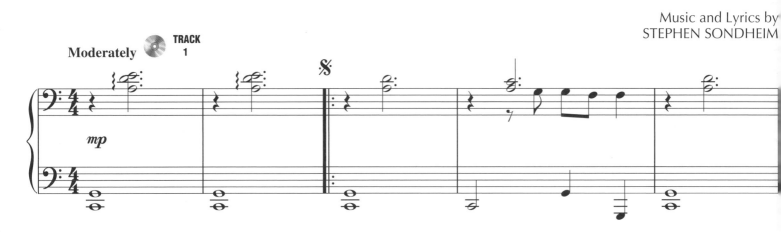

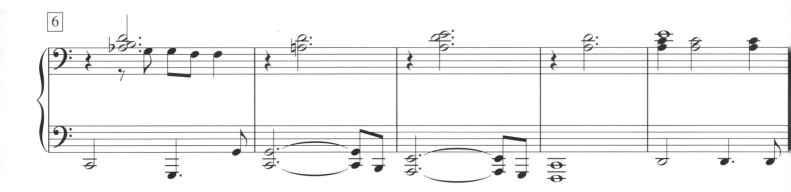

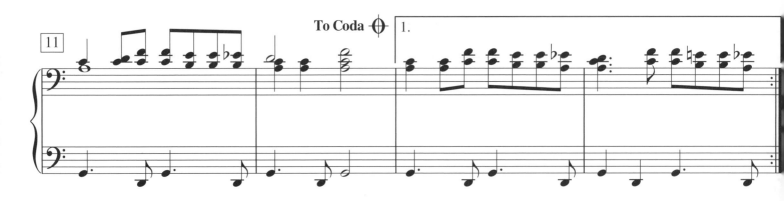

BEING ALIVE
from COMPANY

PRIMO

Music and Lyrics by
STEPHEN SONDHEIM

SECONDO

BROADWAY BABY

from FOLLIES

SECONDO

Music and Lyrics by
STEPHEN SONDHEIM

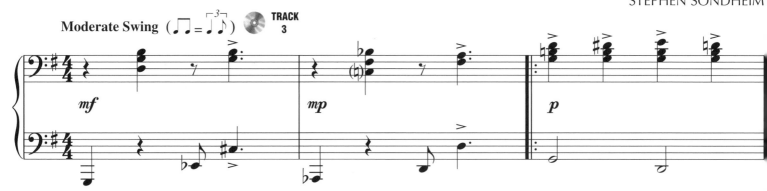

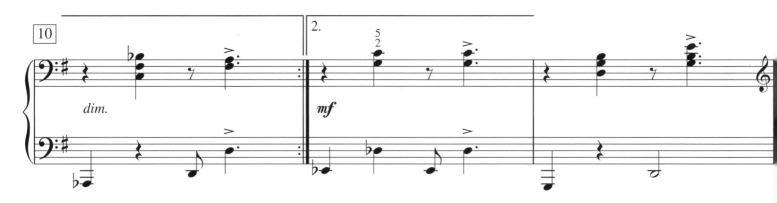

BROADWAY BABY
from FOLLIES

PRIMO

Music and Lyrics by
STEPHEN SONDHEIM

SECONDO

SECONDO

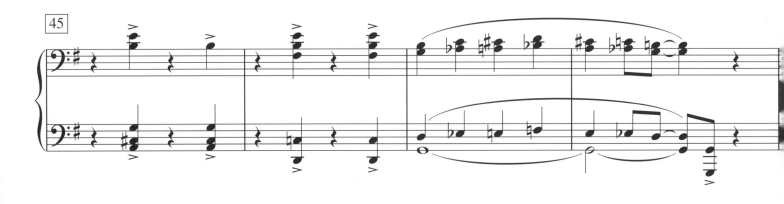

CHILDREN WILL LISTEN
from INTO THE WOODS

SECONDO

Words and Music by
STEPHEN SONDHEIM

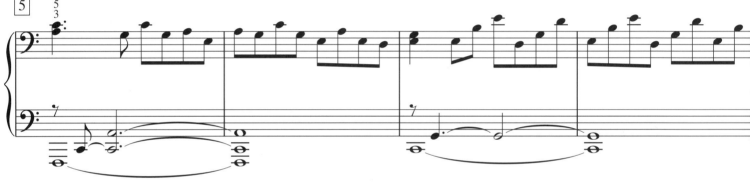

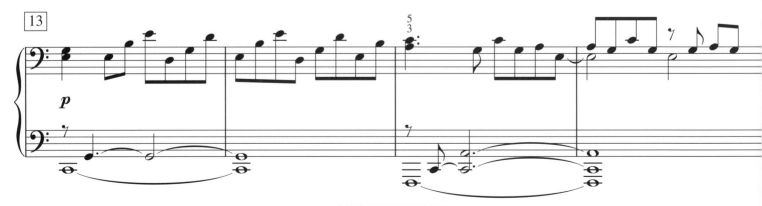

CHILDREN WILL LISTEN
from INTO THE WOODS

PRIMO

Words and Music by
STEPHEN SONDHEIM

Steady (♩ = ca. 100) TRACK 6

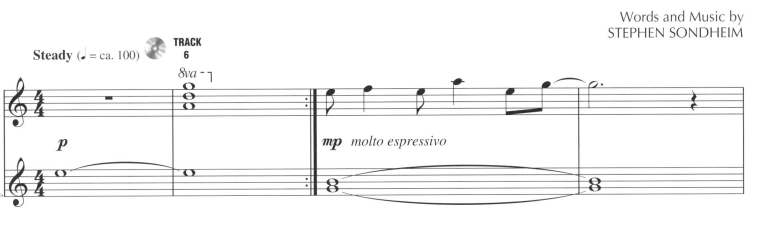

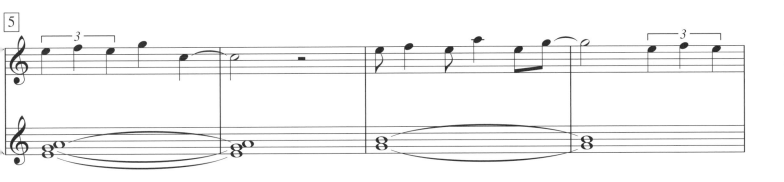

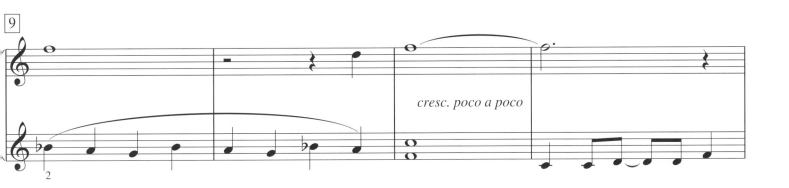

SECONDO

SECONDO

PRIMO

COMEDY TONIGHT
from A FUNNY THING HAPPENED ON THE WAY TO THE FORUM

SECONDO

Words and Music by
STEPHEN SONDHEIM

Brightly TRACK 7

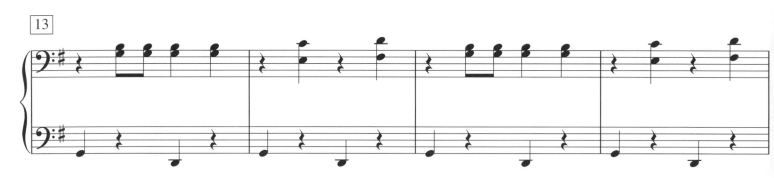

COMEDY TONIGHT
from A FUNNY THING HAPPENED ON THE WAY TO THE FORUM

PRIMO

Words and Music by
STEPHEN SONDHEIM

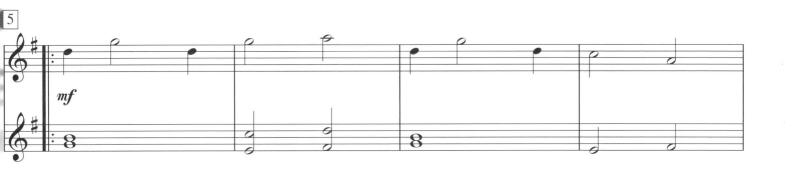

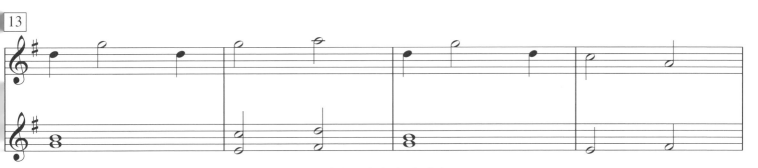

SECONDO

SECONDO

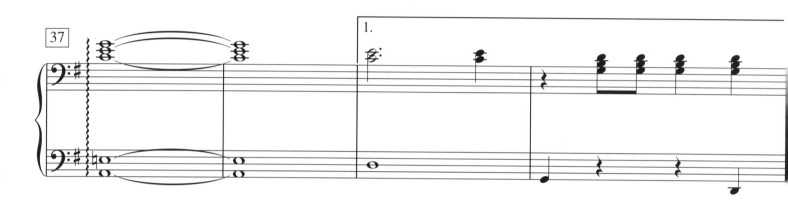

PRIMO

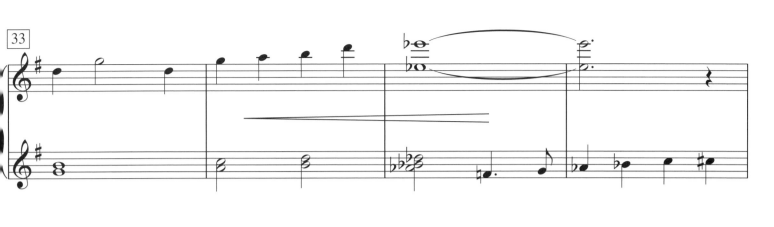

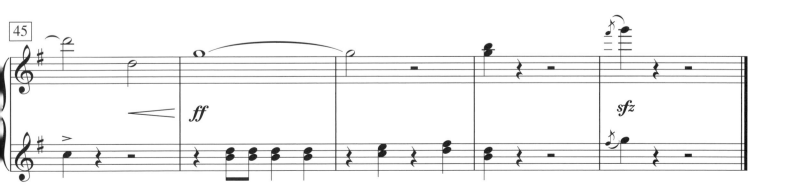

JOHANNA
from SWEENEY TODD

SECONDO

Words and Music by
STEPHEN SONDHEIM

Tranquillo, in 2   TRACK 9

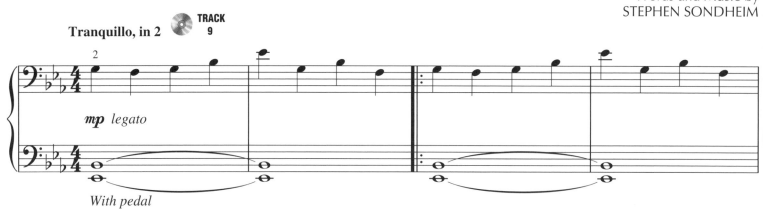

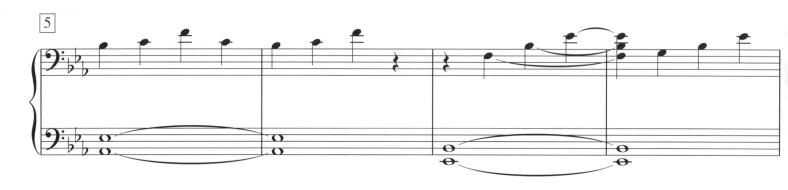

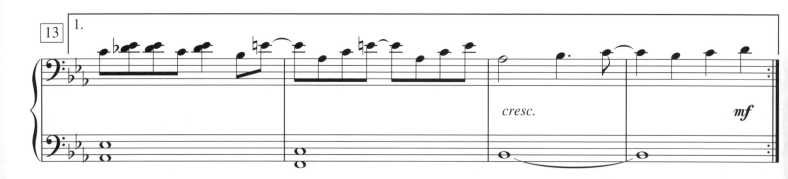

JOHANNA
from SWEENEY TODD

PRIMO

Words and Music by
STEPHEN SONDHEIM

SECONDO

PRIMO

NIGHT WALTZ
from A LITTLE NIGHT MUSIC

SECONDO

Words and Music by
STEPHEN SONDHEIM

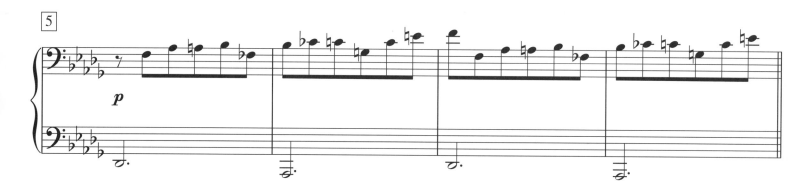

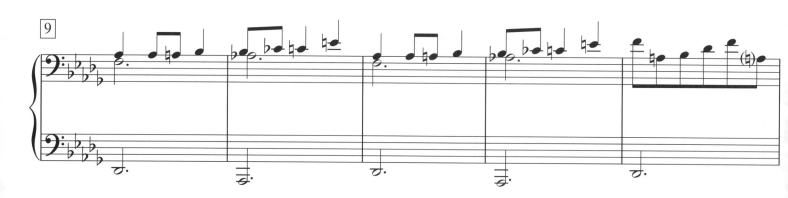

NIGHT WALTZ
from A LITTLE NIGHT MUSIC

PRIMO

Words and Music by
STEPHEN SONDHEIM

SECONDO

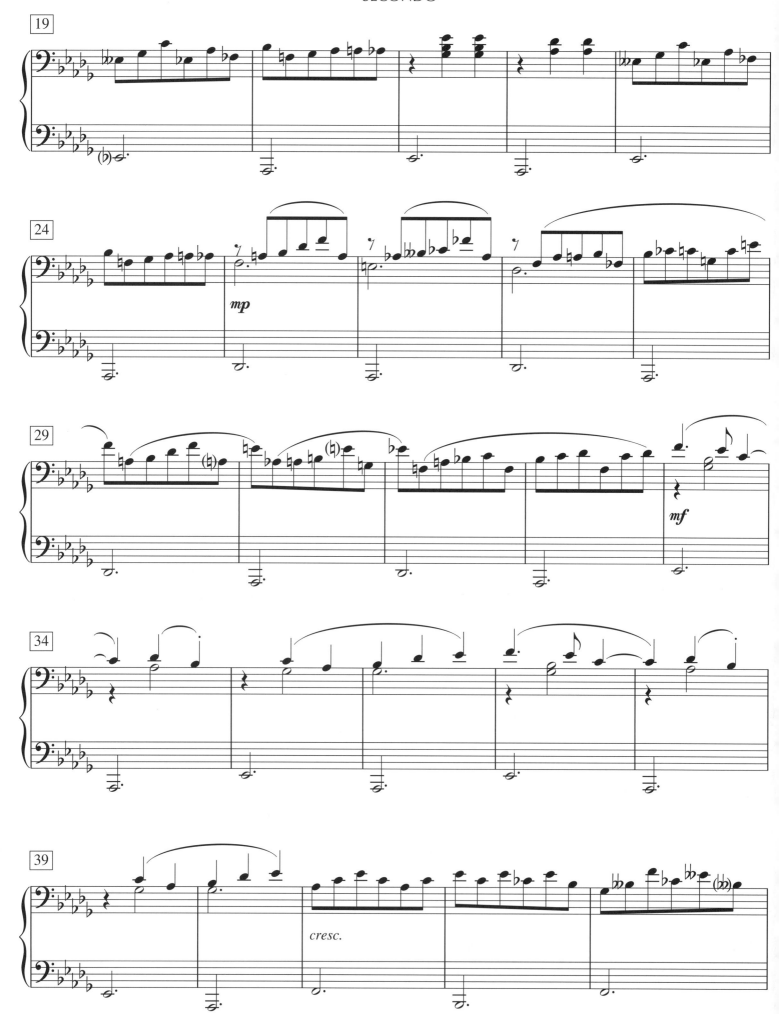

PRIMO

SECONDO

PRIMO

NOT WHILE I'M AROUND

from SWEENEY TODD

SECONDO

Words and Music by
STEPHEN SONDHEIM

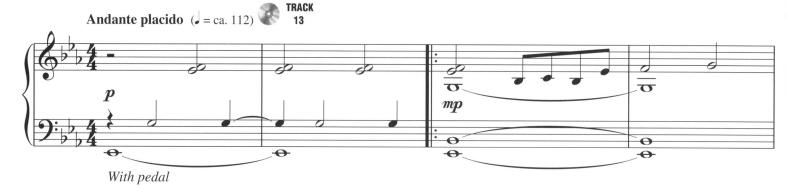

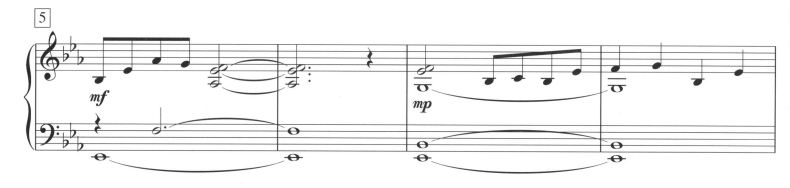

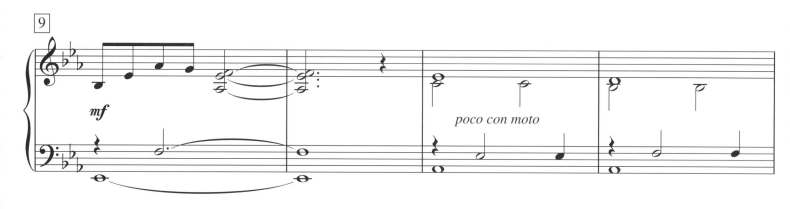

NOT WHILE I'M AROUND

from SWEENEY TODD

PRIMO

Words and Music by
STEPHEN SONDHEIM

Andante placido (♩ = ca. 112) TRACK 14

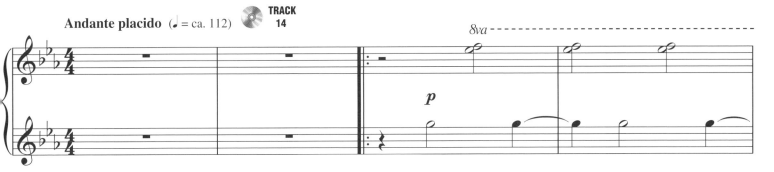

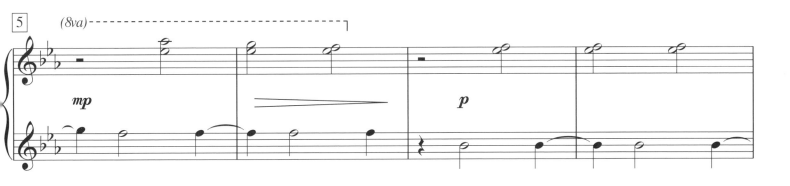

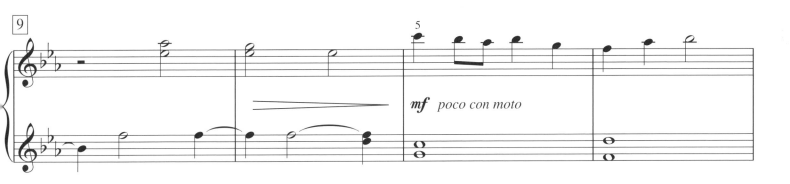

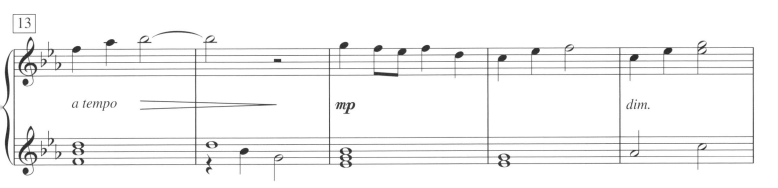

SECONDO

OLD FRIENDS
from MERRILY WE ROLL ALONG

SECONDO

Words and Music by
STEPHEN SONDHEIM

Moderato, in 2 (♩ = ca. 84) 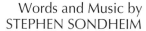 **TRACK 15**

OLD FRIENDS
from MERRILY WE ROLL ALONG

PRIMO

Words and Music by
STEPHEN SONDHEIM

Moderato, in 2 (♩ = ca. 84) TRACK 16

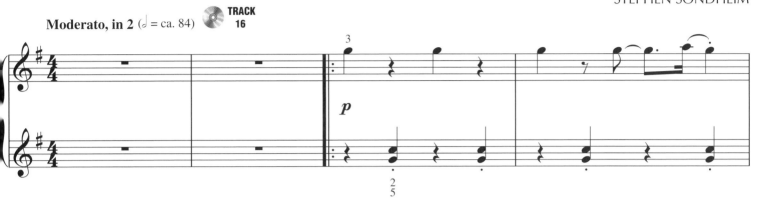

PRIMO

SECONDO

PRIMO

PRETTY WOMEN
from SWEENEY TODD

SECONDO

Words and Music by
STEPHEN SONDHEIM

Languid, but steady; non rubato (♩ = ca. 72)

TRACK 17

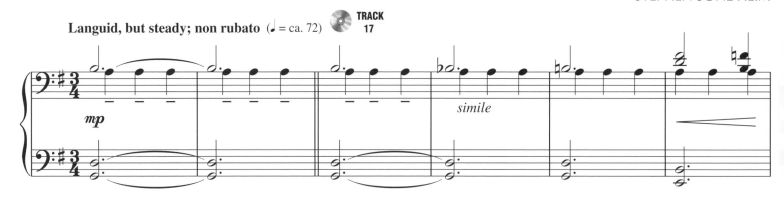

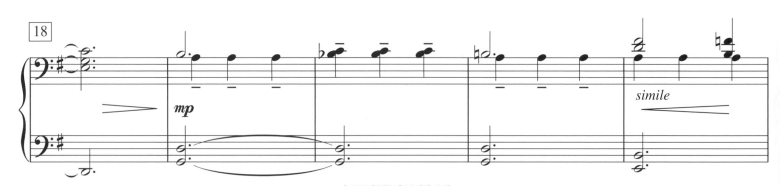

PRETTY WOMEN
from SWEENEY TODD

PRIMO

Words and Music by
STEPHEN SONDHEIM

Languid, but steady; non rubato (♩ = ca. 72)   TRACK 18

SECONDO

PRIMO

SEND IN THE CLOWNS

from A LITTLE NIGHT MUSIC

SECONDO

Words and Music by
STEPHEN SONDHEIM

Moderately slow, with rubato   TRACK 19

SEND IN THE CLOWNS
from A LITTLE NIGHT MUSIC

PRIMO

Words and Music by
STEPHEN SONDHEIM

Moderately slow, with rubato TRACK 20

SECONDO

PRIMO

Piano For Two

A VARIETY OF PIANO DUETS FROM HAL LEONARD

LI – THE BEATLES PIANO DUETS – 2ND EDITION
Features 8 arrangements: Can't Buy Me Love • Eleanor Rigby • Hey Jude • Let It Be • Penny Lane • Something • When I'm Sixty-Four • Yesterday.

00290496..$10.95

I – BROADWAY DUETS
9 duet arrangements of Broadway favorites, including: Cabaret • Comedy Tonight • Ol' Man River • One • and more.

00292077 ....$12.99

LI – BROADWAY FAVORITES
A show-stopping collection of 8 songs arranged as piano duets. Includes: I Dreamed a Dream • If Ever I Would Leave You • Memory • People.

00290185 ....$9.95

LI – COLLECTED SACRED CLASSICS
Arranged by Bill Boyd
8 classics for piano duet, including: Ave Maria • A Mighty Fortress • Hallelujah from *Messiah* • and more.

00221009 ....$9.95

I – DISNEY DUETS
8 songs: Candle on the Water • Colors of the Wind • Cruella de Vil • Hakuna Matata • Someday • A Spoonful of Sugar • Winnie the Pooh • Zip-A-Dee-Doo-Dah.

00290484 ....$12.95

LI – DISNEY MOVIE HITS FOR TWO
9 fun favorites, including: Be Our Guest • Circle of Life • Friend like Me • Under the Sea • A Whole New World • and more.

00292076 ....$14.95

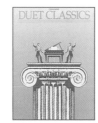

LI – DUET CLASSICS FOR PIANO
8 classical melodies, arranged as piano duets. Includes: Liebestraum (Liszt) • Minuet In G (Beethoven) • Sleeping Beauty Waltz (Tchaikovsky) • and more.

00290172 ....$6.95

LI – GERSHWIN PIANO DUETS
These duet arrangements of 10 Gershwin classics such as "I Got Plenty of Nuttin'," "Summertime," "It Ain't Necessarily So," and "Love Walked In" sound as full and satisfying as the orchestral originals.

00312603 ....$10.95

I – GREAT MOVIE THEMES
8 movie hits, including: Chariots of Fire • Colors of the Wind • The Entertainer • *Forrest Gump – Main Title* • Theme from *Jurassic Park* • Somewhere in Time • Somewhere, My Love • *Star Trek® – The Motion Picture* • and more.

00290494 ....$9.95

UI – LOVE DUETS
7 songs: All I Ask of You • Can You Feel the Love Tonight • Can't Help Falling in Love • Here, There, and Everywhere • Unchained Melody • When I Fall in Love • A Whole New World (Aladdin's Theme).

00290485 ....$8.95

LI – ANDREW LLOYD WEBBER PIANO DUETS
arr. Ann Collins
8 easy piano duets, featuring some of Andrew Lloyd Webber's biggest hits such as: All I Ask of You • Don't Cry for Me Argentina • Memory • I Don't Know How to Love Him.

00290332 ....$12.95

I – MOVIE DUETS
9 songs, including: Chariots of Fire • *The Godfather* (Love Theme) • *Romeo and Juliet* (Love Theme) • Theme from *Schindler's List* • and more.

00292078 ....$9.95

UI – COLE PORTER PIANO DUETS
What a better way to play these 6 Cole Porter love songs such as "Do I Love You?" "I Love Paris," "In The Still of the Night," than with a partner?

00312680..........................$9.95

UI – ROCK 'N' ROLL – PIANO DUETS
Ten early rock classics, including: Blue Suede Shoes • Don't Be Cruel • Rock Around the Clock • Shake, Rattle and Roll.

00290171..........................$9.95

I – THE SOUND OF MUSIC
9 songs, including: Do-Re-Mi • Edelweiss • My Favorite Things • The Sound of Music • and more.

00290389......................$12.95

GRADING
LI = Lower Intermediate
I = Intermediate
UI = Upper Intermediate

FOR MORE INFORMATION, SEE YOUR LOCAL MUSIC DEALER, OR WRITE TO:

HAL•LEONARD®
CORPORATION
7777 W. BLUEMOUND RD. P.O. BOX 13819 MILWAUKEE, WI 53213

www.halleonard.com

PIANO DUETS

The **Piano Duet Play-Along** series is an excellent source for 1 Piano, 4 Hand duets in every genre! It also gives you the flexibility to rehearse or perform piano duets anytime, anywhere! Play these delightful tunes with a partner, or use the accompanying CDs to play along with either the Secondo or Primo part on your own. The CD is enhanced so PC and Mac users can adjust the recording to any tempo without changing pitch.

  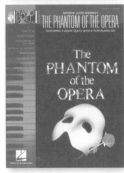

1. Piano Favorites
00290546 Book/CD Pack $14.95

2. Movie Favorites
00290547 Book/CD Pack $14.95

3. Broadway for Two
00290548 Book/CD Pack $14.95

4. The Music of Andrew Lloyd Webber™
00290549 Book/CD Pack $14.95

5. Disney Favorites
00290550 Book/CD Pack $14.95

6. Disney Songs
00290551 Book/CD Pack $14.95

7. Classical Music
00290552 Book/CD Pack $14.95

8. Christmas Classics
00290554 Book/CD Pack $14.95

9. Hymns
00290556 Book/CD Pack $14.95

10. The Sound of Music
00290557 Book/CD Pack $17.99

11. Disney Early Favorites
00290558 Book/CD Pack $16.95

12. Disney Movie Songs
00290559 Book/CD Pack $16.95

13. Movie Hits
00290560 Book/CD Pack $14.95

14. Les Misérables
00290561 Book/CD Pack $16.95

15. God Bless America® & Other Songs for a Better Nation
00290562 Book/CD Pack $14.99

16. Disney Classics
00290563 Book/CD Pack $16.95

17. High School Musical
00290564 Book/CD Pack $16.95

18. High School Musical 2
00290565 Book/CD Pack $16.99

19. Pirates of the Caribbean
00290566 Book/CD Pack $16.95

20. Wicked
00290567 Book/CD Pack $16.99

21. Peanuts®
00290568 Book/CD Pack $16.99

22. Rodgers & Hammerstein
00290569 Book/CD Pack $14.99

23. Cole Porter
00290570 Book/CD Pack $14.99

24. Christmas Carols
00290571 Book/CD Pack $14.95

25. Wedding Songs
00290572 Book/CD Pack $14.99

26. Love Songs
00290573 Book/CD Pack $14.99

27. Romantic Favorites
00290574 Book/CD Pack $14.99

28. Classical for Two
00290575 Book/CD Pack $14.99

29. Broadway Classics
00290576 Book/CD Pack $14.99

30. Jazz Standards
00290577 Book/CD Pack $14.99

31. Pride and Prejudice
00290578 Book/CD Pack $14.99

32. Sondheim for Two
00290579 Book/CD Pack $16.99

33. Twilight
00290580 Book/CD Pack $14.99

34. Hannah Montana
00290581 Book/CD Pack $16.99

35. High School Musical 3
00290582 Book/CD Pack $16.99

36. Holiday Favorites
00290583 Book/CD Pack $14.99

37. Christmas for Two
00290584 Book/CD Pack $14.99

38. Lennon & McCartney Favorites
00290585 Book/CD Pack $14.99

39. Lennon & McCartney Hits
00290586 Book/CD Pack $14.99

40. Classical Themes
00290588 Book/CD Pack $14.99

41. The Phantom of the Opera
00290589 Book/CD Pack $16.99

42. Glee
00290590 Book/CD Pack $16.99

FOR MORE INFORMATION, SEE YOUR LOCAL MUSIC DEALER, OR WRITE TO:

7777 W. BLUEMOUND RD. P.O. BOX 13819 MILWAUKEE, WI 53213

Visit Hal Leonard Online at **www.halleonard.com**

0810